How to use this book

This Year 6 Handwriting workbook is matched to the National Curriculum and is designed to improve handwriting skills.

Activities split into three levels of difficulty – **Challenge 1**, **Challenge 2** and **Challenge 3** – to help progression.

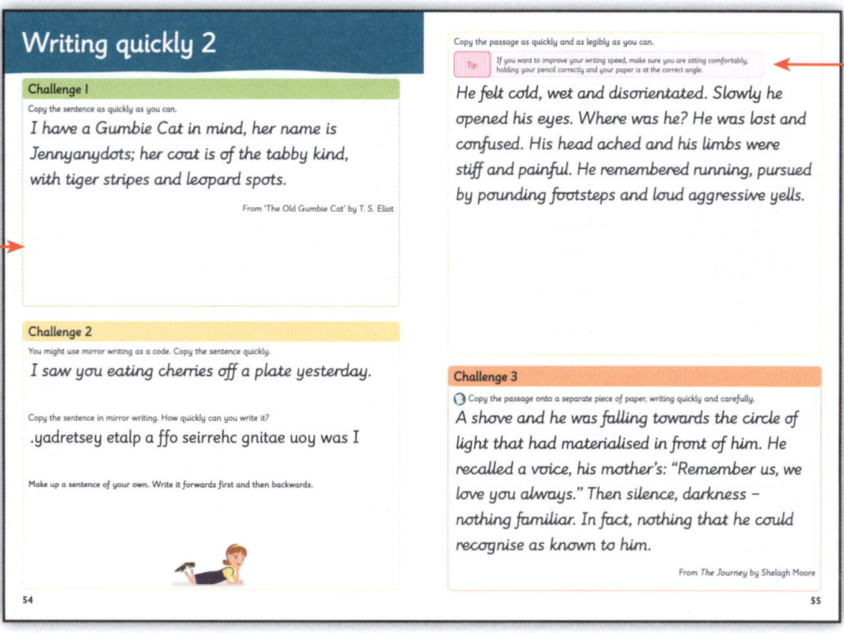

Writing quickly 2

Challenge 1

Copy the sentence as quickly as you can.

I have a Gumbie Cat in mind, her name is Jennyanydots; her coat is of the tabby kind, with tiger stripes and leopard spots.

From 'The Old Gumbie Cat' by T. S. Eliot

Challenge 2

You might use mirror writing as a code. Copy the sentence quickly.

I saw you eating cherries off a plate yesterday.

Copy the sentence in mirror writing. How quickly can you write it?

.yadretsey etalp a ffo seirrehc gnitae uoy was I

Make up a sentence of your own. Write it forwards first and then backwards.

54

Copy the passage as quickly and as legibly as you can.

Tip: If you want to improve your writing speed, make sure you are sitting comfortably, holding your pencil correctly and your paper is at the correct angle.

He felt cold, wet and disorientated. Slowly he opened his eyes. Where was he? He was lost and confused. His head ached and his limbs were stiff and painful. He remembered running, pursued by pounding footsteps and loud aggressive yells.

Challenge 3

Copy the passage onto a separate piece of paper, writing quickly and carefully.

A shove and he was falling towards the circle of light that had materialised in front of him. He recalled a voice, his mother's: "Remember us, we love you always." Then silence, darkness – nothing familiar. In fact, nothing that he could recognise as known to him.

From *The Journey* by Shelagh Moore

55

Handy **tips** are included throughout.

Starter check recaps skills already learned.

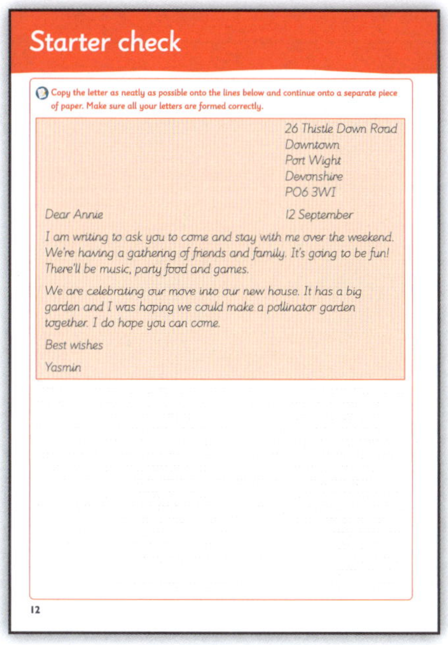

Starter check

Copy the letter as neatly as possible onto the lines below and continue onto a separate piece of paper. Make sure all your letters are formed correctly.

26 Thistle Down Road
Downtown
Port Wight
Devonshire
PO6 3WI

Dear Annie

12 September

I am writing to ask you to come and stay with me over the weekend. We're having a gathering of friends and family. It's going to be fun! There'll be music, party food and games.

We are celebrating our move into our new house. It has a big garden and I was hoping we could make a pollinator garden together. I do hope you can come.

Best wishes

Yasmin

12

Four **Progress checks** included throughout the book for ongoing assessment and monitoring progress.

Progress check 2

1. Write notes which list the key points of the phone message.

"Hi Arif, so, um... let's meet. Yeah, let's go to the Highways Coffee House. Yeah, there at, um, 2pm. No, 3pm. Yeah. It's on Water Lane. Yeah. Tomorrow. Right?"

2. Copy the sentences, making sure your joins are correct.

Please do not disappear while I am arranging your places.

At night, the town was vividly lit with bright lights.

Put your rulers down on the windowsill.

50

Contents

ACKNOWLEDGEMENTS

Published by Collins
An imprint of HarperCollins*Publishers* Ltd
1 London Bridge Street
London SE1 9GF

HarperCollins*Publishers*
Macken House
39/40 Mayor Street Upper
Dublin 1
D01 C9W8
Ireland

ISBN 978-0-00-853469-1

First published 2023

10 9 8 7 6 5 4 3 2 1

P.39 'Transformations' by Tadeusz Różewicz, from The Survivors and Other Poems. Published by Princeton University Press; P.59 'The ABC' by Spike Milligan. © Spike Milligan. Used by kind permission of Spike Milligan Productions.

British Library Cataloguing in Publication Data.

A CIP record of this book is available from the British Library.

Publishers: Fiona McGlade and Jennifer Hall
Author: Shelagh Moore

Series Editor: Dr Jane Medwell
Project Management and Editorial: Chantal Addy
Cover Design: Sarah Duxbury
Inside Concept Design: Ian Wrigley
Typesetting and Artwork: Jouve India Private Limited
Production: Emma Wood
Printed in India by Multivista Global Pvt. Ltd

MIX
Paper | Supporting responsible forestry
FSC www.fsc.org FSC™ C007454

This book is produced from independently certified FSC™ paper to ensure responsible forest management.

For more information visit: www.harpercollins.co.uk/green

Guidance for parents

Handwriting at home – Year 6

Handwriting that is efficient, fluent and readable is the basis of successful writing – it allows children to compose what they want to say. Handwriting helps children to learn a range of important aspects of the curriculum. Parental support can make a huge difference to a child's handwriting development – a few minutes of daily practice can make all the difference.

Year 6 priorities are to:

- practise controlling the size and relative proportions of letters
- learn to make the trickier joins between letters automatically and smoothly
- be able to write quickly, but legibly
- learn to make choices about when to "speed up" their writing, with the inevitable trade off with neatness, but retaining legibility
- choose the correct writing tool for the job
- learn to print in lower-case and in block capitals, when appropriate
- use the names and alphabetical order of the letters to order items
- develop their own style of writing by slanting their writing.

The aim of handwriting in Year 6 is to enable children to choose the speed and style of their writing to suit the task. In this workbook we have included some longer pieces of writing to copy. This will require some additional paper, ideally lined.

Not all children will learn with the same level of ease or at the same rate. In Year 6, children who struggle with automatic letter production or joining may find that their handwriting hinders their access to the curriculum or inhibits composition. Where this is the case, practice of the letter movements and joins should be the focus of using this workbook.

The first section of this workbook focuses on practising some of the content from Year 5, which will be developed in Year 6. Throughout the workbook your child will practise the five main types of joins:

1. Diagonal joins to letters without ascenders (for example: *ai*)
2. Diagonal joins to letters with ascenders (for example: *ch*)
3. Horizontal joins to letters without ascenders (for example: *wa*)
4. Horizontal joins to letters with ascenders (for example: *wh*)
5. Joins to round (anti-clockwise) letters (for example: *ad*).

KS2 writers need to remember not to join break letters b, g, j, p, q, x, y, z and s because this allows them to write with maximum efficiency. This workbook asks your child to do some careful writing, with an emphasis on neatness, and some writing at speed, where neatness is not the main priority but the writing must be legible. The tasks address tricky joins, the relative sizing of letters, the spacing of punctuation and spaces between words, and puts practice of these writing issues in the context of both fast and neat writing.

The workbook also includes practice of capital letters (which never join), alphabetical order and punctuation. The proofreading exercises promote scrutiny of their own text. The workbook focuses on words children need to learn in their spelling practice (from the National Curriculum list) and some grammar and punctuation issues, helping them to make the most of their practice time.

Writing tools and holding a pen or pencil

If your child has mastered all the letters, they can choose to use any writing tool. An ordinary "lead" pencil has a good combination of grip and slip and is especially suited to notes and informal texts. By Year 6, most children like to use pens and, in this case, we recommend fibre-tipped handwriting pens because they offer the best combination of friction and slip. Fibre-tipped pens are very controllable, as are ballpoint pens which use liquid ink; both are good tools to practise with. Ballpoint pens which use slippery, viscous ink are very hard to control and we would not recommend them for learners. Fountain pens are a novelty writing tool, but one which gives many learners a great deal of satisfaction and fun.

Traditionally, we expect children to hold the pencil between the thumb and index finger with the pencil supported on the middle finger. However, this is not the only successful pencil grip, and the important thing is to find a grip that provides comfort, stability and control. Aim for your child to have control of the writing tool but not to grip it too hard, as this will tire their hands, arms and even their shoulders. If you think your child is gripping the pen too hard ask them to cup a ball of loosely scrunched up paper (about the diameter of a 10 pence piece) in the palm of their writing hand while they hold the pen. This helps relax the hand. It is also important for children to regularly put down the pen and give their writing hands a wriggle.

Left-handed children

Although most children are right-handed, around 10 percent of any population is left-handed.

Left-handed children may like to sit on slightly higher chairs and hold the writing tool slightly further from the point, to cope with the demands of letters designed for right handers. It is harder for left-handed children to use a fountain pen neatly, because the nib may dig into the paper.

Practising handwriting and self-evaluation

With practice, your child will "feel" the correct letter movement or join and develop fluent and even handwriting. We recommend frequent short practice sessions of 5-15 minutes especially for children who are struggling with the formation of any letter, or with developing speed. Though this does not sound like much, a few minutes a day really can make a positive difference.

When your child uses this workbook for handwriting practice, they should slant the page to maintain a good writing position. Left-handers usually slant the top of the page to the right and right-handers slant the top of the page to the left. This is good practice. If your child can sit at a table to write, it will help them get used to doing this.

Talking with your child about their handwriting practice is very helpful and can easily be overlooked towards the end of KS2. The "self-evaluation grids" in the "progress checks" are designed to help you discuss your child's progress at handwriting. The "progress chart" on the last page allows your child to record how they feel about their handwriting after completing the workbook. It is always good to notice and praise efforts or improvements as it helps your child become confident and proud of their handwriting.

Warm up and revise

Copy the words as quickly and carefully as you can.

Tip Make your quick writing legible.

achieve achieve achieve

curiosity

interrupt

Copy the sentences, taking care to leave space for the punctuation marks.

P.O. stands for Post Office.

B.B.C. stands for British Broadcasting Corporation.

U.K. means the United Kingdom.

“Please close the door,” Dad said, “it’s very cold tonight; we want to keep the heat in.”

Copy the sentences, putting in the capital letters.

“i’d like to see ‘the lost city’ at the cinema,” said sara.

we live in the united kingdom.

Copy the sentences, putting in the speech marks that are needed.

Please, please let me have another ride, begged Bill.

You have had four turns already, replied his dad.

Copy the list, putting in commas where needed.

I went to the shops and bought a lot of butter eggs flour and chocolate to bake a cake.

How I feel about...			
my capital letters in sentences			
my abbreviations			
adding punctuation			

Warm up and revise

Copy the words, putting them in alphabetical order.

Hint Remember the rule if the words begin with the same letter.

mischief January opportunity
occur marvellous jury

Copy the sentence, remembering how to join and from f.

Flopsy the bunny raced around the garden, carefully jumping fifty times over the flowers.

Copy the sentence, remembering how to join to and from r.

Running around the track was tiring but he wanted to qualify for the final race.

Think about your diagonal and horizontal joins. Copy the words and sentence.

lightning

temperature

thunder

storm

A large parcel arrived at the yacht for the Captain.

Copy the sentence, making sure your ascenders and descenders are straight up or down.

Hovering above the clouds, the balloon banged and bounced about in the fast-flowing air currents.

Write the contraction next to the words. The first one has been done for you.

you would ___you'd___

will not ______________

should not ______________

she has ______________

would not ______________

you have ______________

we are ______________

How I feel about...	😐	🙂	😃
putting words in alphabetical order			
writing contractions			
my horizontal and diagonal joins			

Warm up and revise

Print the labels on the diagram using the words in the box. Remember, printing does not join.

wheel	pedal	handlebar	saddle	frame

Copy the note quickly.

To: All staff   Date: 22 December   From: May

Sorry, Christmas party cancelled. Will now be held after Christmas.

Copy the address neatly and tidily.

77 Surrey Road

Lincoln

Lincolnshire

LI7 4ON

Copy the words then complete the sentences by writing the words in the correct places.

pedestrians

hexagon

domicile

century

A __________ lasts for a hundred years.

Another word for your home is __________.

__________ do not travel on bikes, in cars or on scooters; they walk.

There are six sides in a __________.

Copy the poem as quickly and carefully as you can onto a separate piece of paper.

When Betty eats spaghetti,
She slurps, she slurps, she slurps,
And when she's finished slurping,
She burps, she burps, she burps.

'When Betty Eats Spaghetti' by Colin West

How I feel about...			
spacing letters			
printing labels			
writing quickly and neatly			

Starter check

Copy the letter as neatly as possible onto the lines below and continue onto a separate piece of paper. Make sure all your letters are formed correctly.

26 Thistle Down Road
Downtown
Port Wight
Devonshire
PO6 3WI

Dear Annie

12 September

I am writing to ask you to come and stay with me over the weekend. We're having a gathering of friends and family. It's going to be fun! There'll be music, party food and games.

We are celebrating our move into our new house. It has a big garden and I was hoping we could make a pollinator garden together. I do hope you can come.

Best wishes

Yasmin

Copy the passage, putting in the correct punctuation.

Tip There are five sentences, one with speech marks.

i woke up feeling really groggy looking out of the the window I saw the trees bending in the wind the rain was pounding down on the roof no wonder I felt groggy dad I yelled theres a fallen tree in the garden.

On a separate piece of paper, write as many words about your birthday as you can in 30 seconds. Underline any words you think are not easy to read.

How I feel about...	😐	🙂	😀
my neatest writing			
my layout of a letter			
my spacing of punctuation			

My handwriting: writing quickly and neatly

Challenge 1

Copy the words as neatly as you can.

correspond

privilege

vegetable

Copy the words again as quickly as you can. Underline any words that are not as neat as above.

correspond

privilege

vegetable

Challenge 2

Copy the sentences quickly and neatly. Underline the proper nouns.

Gianna and Matteo walked along the track.

It was a cold day and they were dressed in warm clothes.

They were walking in Mere Forest Country Park, which was a lovely forest with lots of trees in it.

The sentences are written backwards. Write them forwards.

Tip You might find it helpful to write the sentence in rough first and then copy it again correcting any mistakes.

.pihs eht gnicaf, edisyauq eht no sdnats enarc ehT

.kcurt a otno ograc eht ecalp edisyauq eht no nem ehT

Challenge 3

Copy the poem as quickly and neatly as you can onto a separate piece of paper.

Swift things are beautiful;
Swallows and deer,
And lightning that falls
Bright-veined and clear,
Rivers and meteors,
Wind in the wheat,
The strong-withered horse,
The runner's sure feet.

From 'Swift Things are Beautiful' by Elizabeth Coatsworth

Developing your own style and writing f

Challenge 1

Copy the sentences carefully, joining the letter f to other letters where you can. Will you use a diagonal or horizontal join?

Farook focused on finding a familiar flower.

Helpful Frank was feeling awful.

At the fair, the ferris wheel ground to a familiar halt.

Fido was a fluffy, friendly pup.

Look at your writing of letter f and underline the joined fs you liked best.

Challenge 2

Here is an example of a tongue twister using the letter f. Copy it neatly.

Four friendly friends flew fast.

Make up and write two tongue twisters of your own using the letter f. Can you say them quickly?

Copy the passage, writing the letter f in your own style.

"Please don't throw away the leftovers, we can feed them to those in need." Sofia faithfully collected the leftovers as she felt food should not be wasted. She emerged from the kitchen and faced the queue waiting for their food.

Challenge 3

Copy the sentences as neatly as you can onto a separate piece of paper using your own style.

Flo liked the foliage flourishing in the flowerbed.

The fugitive fled from difficult foes.

Frank found it sufficiently feasible.

The curfew was set for half past four.

12
1
2
3
4
5
6
7
8
9
10
11

Joining to and from r

Challenge 1

Copy the words, joining the letter r to other letters.

very

restaurant

refreshment

Copy the sentence.

Rollicking, roistering pirates sailed across the sea, raiding as their fancy took them.

Challenge 2

Copy the sentences. Make sure your letter rs are joined correctly.

Ralph the Rover reflected on his target to raid and plunder for treasure.

Unfortunately, his hired ship was lost in a storm with all the treasure and Ralph as well!

Write the words from the box next to the correct definitions.

Tip You can use your dictionary to check you are correct.

correspond	prejudice	research	narrative

to investigate facts, to collect information on a subject.

an account of events or a story.

to communicate, usually by writing to someone.

intolerance or dislike of people because of who they are or an opinion that you have formed about something or someone.

Challenge 3

Copy the short extract.

And the wretched Council's bosoms beat,
As the Piper turn'd from the High Street
To where the Weser roll'd its waters
Right in the way of their sons and daughters!

From 'The Pied Piper of Hamelin' by Robert Browning

Slanting key joins: diagonal joins

Challenge 1

Copy the words carefully, slanting your writing.

logical

upset

underdone

sheep

Copy the sentences, slanting your writing.

The community had to rebuild the shepherd's hut and fence the field. They needed to keep the sheep safe from wolves.

Challenge 2

Copy the sentences, filling in the missing words from the list.

trick	*clever*	*flipped*	*developed*	*successfully*

The magician ______________ *his magic* ______________.

He ____________ the coin ____________ to make it disappear from one hand and reappear in the other hand.

He was a ____________ magician.

Write two sentences using some of the words in the box on the previous page.

Challenge 3

Copy the lines onto a separate piece of paper.

Jibber, jabber, gabble, babble
Cackle, clack and prate,
Twiddle, twaddle, mutter, stutter,
Utter, splutter, blate.

From 'What Some People Do' by Anonymous

Keeping ascenders and descenders parallel

Challenge 1

Copy the letters.

g p q l t d

f h j k y

Copy the sentence, making sure that your descenders and ascenders are parallel.

Felicity had quarrelled with her brother; she felt quite sad afterwards, and so did her brother.

Challenge 2

Copy the passage.

"Please don't throw away the leftovers, we can feed them to those in need." Sofia painstakingly collected them as she abhorred waste. She emerged from the kitchen with her implements washed, ready to put away.

Make up two tongue twisters using the letters **p** and **h**.

Challenge 3

Copy the verse, which uses different ascenders and descenders, as neatly as you can.

Chatter, patter, tattle, prattle,
Chew the rag and crack,
Spiel and spout and spit it out,
Tell the world and quack.

From 'What Some People Do' by Anonymous

Placing and spacing punctuation: sentence types

Challenge 1

Copy the sentences, adding the correct punctuation at the end of each one. Identify whether the sentence is a question, a command, an exclamation or a statement.

Do not run in the corridor

I walked to town yesterday

Are you tired

Look, look – there's a rainbow

Challenge 2

Copy the simple and complex (compound) sentences, putting in any punctuation that is needed.

james wanted to draw a picture of his dog

my friends phoned me they wanted to meet up at the park

i want to go home

theres a park across the road go and have a picnic there

Copy the sentences and punctuate them carefully.

there is a space behind the door for your umbrella

tell me where the classroom is located

what is your name

look out there's a car coming

Challenge 3

Copy the passage onto a separate piece of paper. Underline the command sentence.

There was a boy who enjoyed walking in the rain. One day, he was walking and it began to rain. Wow, rain! As he walked, his new jumper got very wet and soggy. When he got home, his mother said, "Take off that wet jumper at once." When his jumper had dried, it had shrunk and was too small for him.

Writing quickly 1

Challenge 1

Writing quickly is important as your writing skills improve. Copy the words, making sure they are correctly spelt and clearly written.

opportunity parliament relevant

environment queue competition

Copy the words as quickly as you can, timing yourself.

opportunity parliament relevant

environment queue competition

I wrote the words in ________ seconds.

Challenge 2

Copy the passage quickly, making sure all the words are copied correctly.

Rashid walked quickly along the path. He was looking for a special track he had discovered the other day. Suddenly, he came across it and started to run down the track. He didn't want to be late for the meeting.

How long did it take you to copy the passage? ________ seconds

Challenge 3

Complete this timed challenge by setting a stopwatch and copying the words below quickly and carefully into the correct sentences.

restaurant	meal
marvellous	competition

Simon and Aida had won a ____________.

They felt ____________.

The prize was a special ____________ at the local ____________ in their village.

How long did it take you to copy the words? ________ seconds

Write ten words about the weather. Use the words to write a short paragraph about the weather on a separate piece of paper. How quickly can you do this?

Writing neatly: formal messages

Challenge 1

Copy the message carefully.

Tip Formal messages do not have contractions, abbreviations or slang in them.

To all pupils in Class 6

Please remember to take home all your personal items at the end of term.

Thank you

Mrs Briggs, Headteacher

Challenge 2

Copy out the two formal sentences, ignoring the informal one.

We are happy to let you know that you have been chosen for a part in the school play.

My diary: I didn't like having to sit for so long, it was a real drag!

Please make sure the outside doors are always closed.

Write the correct words from the box into the formal message below.

sincerely opportunity activities
provision individual

Dear Parents,

Please note that the school trip has ample ________ for each ________ to take part in different ________. We hope your child will take the ________ to learn new skills.

Yours ________

J. Jones, Headteacher

Challenge 3

On a separate piece of paper, write your own formal message, inviting a friend to your house for tea. Here are some ideas:

Dear ________

You are ________ to my house for ________.

We will be eating at ________ pm.

With best wishes

Progress check 1

1. Copy the words quickly and neatly.

Tip: Think about speed and your joins.

pronunciation especially awkward desperate

fairness folly sacrifice interfere

ramble roaring forty research

2. Copy the sentences, making sure your joins are correct.

His pronunciation was excellent. In fairness, he was the best speaker in the group. He did not ramble but kept to the point.

3. Copy the passage, making sure your ascenders and descenders are parallel.

The secretary walked into the office with a pile of papers for the committee to approve. They needed signing before posting. The secretary hoped the committee would not take too long to complete the task.

4. Copy and punctuate the sentences carefully. Then draw lines to match them to the type of sentence they are.

go and fetch your coat

are you ready for your meal

look it's snowing

the children worked hard to improve their writing

question

statement

command

exclamation

How I feel about...	😐	🙂	😃
my descenders and ascenders			
using punctuation			
my joins			

Progress check 1

5. Copy the passage, making sure you space the punctuation correctly.

"I am going out to the park today," said Jamila. It was a lovely sunny day and she wanted to have a break outside.

"Come back at once," said her mum. "There's too much work to be done before your cousins arrive."

Jamila scowled – she didn't want to work on a sunny day.

6. Copy as many of the words as you can in one minute. Make sure they are legible.

amateur average bruise correspond
determined dictionary exaggerate
government harass identify language
muscles occur persuade physical queen

quarter quickly repetition secretary

temperature variety willingly yacht zone

7. Copy the message neatly onto a separate piece of paper.

Dear Parents

I'd like to thank you for all your support this year. We're pleased that so many of the pupils achieved their potential in school work, sports, music, art and drama. I'm hoping that they will do well in all their endeavours in their new schools.

Yours sincerely

B. Bloggs, Headteacher

How I feel about...	😐	🙂	😃
my quick writing			
my neat writing			
spacing punctuation correctly			

Writing brief notes about an event

Challenge 1

Write brief notes about what is happening in the picture.

HURRICANE
SEASON

Challenge 2

Read the following passage.

Anita was answering the phone in the office. The phone rang so she answered it.
"Hello, is Madame Francois there?"
Anita replied that Madame was out for the day. The caller asked her to tell Madame that he would be calling on her tomorrow at 10a.m. to discuss the repairs to her roof. He wanted her to have a list of other work she had mentioned to him as well. He would then be able to give her a proper price for the work.

Copy the note Anita left for Madame Francois.

For: Madame Francois Date: 5 April 2022

- Builder coming tomorrow 6 April at 10a.m.
- Roof repairs plus all other jobs to be discussed.
- Price to be decided.

From: Anita

Challenge 3

Write the key events from the following newspaper report in note form on a separate piece of paper.

Maddie Smith, aged 12, from Bolton was walking home from Bolton Academy. She saw a horse pulling a cart trotting down the street without a driver. She ran after the horse, which stopped to eat some grass. Talking to it gently, she led the horse to a safe place and called the police. Inspector Manning said, "Maddie is a brave girl and did all the right things. She is a good rider and knew how to talk to the horse. Don't try this if you don't know about horses though," he advised.

You have been invited to a party. Write a note in your diary to remind yourself about it. Write your note on a separate piece of paper.

Writing notes into full sentences

Challenge 1

Write out the sentences in full, with the abbreviations as full words and using capital letters where needed.

dr jones is a VIP.

C U ltr. Don't forget to wait 4 me.

The ad said it was approx. 4k from here.

Challenge 2

Write the notes out as full sentences.

Party Drink

Need:

1l mixed fruit squash

Water

Fruit/cucumber

Method:

20ml squash per 500ml water

Slice fruit/cucumber

Add ice

Challenge 3

Copy the notes from the interview below as full sentences onto a separate piece of paper.

Who?	Jolyon Jones, singer, 19yrs.
What?	Mega-selling track. Made a million £
Where?	Lives New York. Work mostly LA.
Concert?	October, London, arena

Spacing key joins: horizontal joins

Challenge 1

Continue the letter patterns.

wrwr

veve

wowo

ordord

aveave

aweawe

Copy the words, making sure your horizontal joins are correct.

avenue

arrange

wonder

comb

adventure

awesome

advisor

unwrap

Challenge 2

Copy the passage carefully, thinking about how you are joining your letters.

As I was walking along the road, I saw a fox cub.
As I approached it, I saw it was injured. Taking

off my jacket, I wrapped the fox cub in it and made my way to the local vet's surgery. Fortunately, he was not badly injured. The nurse put Foxy, the name one of the vets gave him, into a cage to rest. They would see he was helped back into the wild when he was ready.

Challenge 3

Copy the verse onto a separate piece of paper.

My little son enters
The room and says
"you are a vulture
I am a mouse"

From 'Transformations' by Tadeusz Różewicz

Joining and breaking descenders

Challenge 1

Copy the break letters with descenders.

Tip These descenders do not join to the next letter.

g j p q y

Copy the passage carefully.

Basher has quickly built a very large sandcastle. It has an excellent moat and a jaunty flag is flapping from its flagpole.

Challenge 2

Write the correct words from the box into the sentences below, then copy the completed sentences.

gigantic	*adjacent*	*April*	*quietly*

It was ________________ *and the snow was falling.*

The snowman was standing ________________ *to the wall in the garden.*

It was a ________________ snowman, much bigger than the little boy who was ________________ admiring it.

Copy the tongue twisters.

Greatly prized Greek grapes grow green or red.

Jolly John jostled Jenny who was making jelly!

Peter Piper picked a peck of pickled peppers – why?

Quack, quack a unique duck squatted on the quay.

Challenge 3

Copy the sentences onto a separate piece of paper. Write two sentences of your own that include the letters g, j, q and y.

My brother plays jokes on us. He just does, he can't help it. Perhaps quite soon my brother might not so we might enjoy some quiet play.

Writing words with qu

Challenge 1

Copy the two letters as many times as you can.

qu

Copy the words and their meanings carefully.

quinquagenarian – a person who is between fifty and fifty-nine years old

demisemiquaver – a musical note

acquisitiveness – great interest in getting money or things

Challenge 2

Copy the sentences containing words beginning with **qu**, thinking carefully about your joins and break letters.

Ducks quack, quails do not.

"Is this the correct quote?" queried the actor.

We really needed to quench our thirst so we waited in the long queue for a drink.

The audience quietened down as the quizmaster began to ask questions.

Challenge 3

Write the correct words from the box into the sentences below, then copy the completed sentences onto a separate piece of paper.

queasy	cheque	squawk
quaking	squib	

The boy threw a firework called a __________ that makes a hissing sound before exploding.

He lent over the side of the boat feeling very __________ indeed.

Mum wrote a __________ to pay for my jacket.

He let out a __________ and stood __________ as the bushes parted.

Break letters: y j g p

Challenge 1

The break letters y, j, g and p do not join to the letters that come after them. Write over and copy the words.

young junior

giraffe potato

mighty unjust

aged opposites

Challenge 2

Copy the sentences.

Our journey was aggravating as we kept having to queue for a place on the boats.

The orchestra was practising the music for the concert; they wanted applause on the night!

Copy the riddles and choose the correct answers from the box below.

January	a coat of paint	an egg

I must be broken before you can use me.

I'm a coat that can go on walls and doors.

I come first but for only thirty-one days.

Challenge 3

Copy the poem onto a separate piece of paper.

Come play with me;
Why should you run
Through the shaking tree
As though I'd a gun
To strike you dead?
When all I would do
Is to scratch your head
And let you go.

'To A Squirrel At Kyle-Na-No' by W. B. Yeats

Placing and spacing punctuation: apostrophes in contractions

Challenge 1

Copy the words and their contractions carefully.

Tip The apostrophe takes the place of a letter and there is a letter gap needed for it. Example: it is – it's

might not – mightn't

must not – mustn't

could not – couldn't

where is – where's

Copy the sentence.

Maisie didn't like cake; she might've enjoyed it if she'd tried it.

Challenge 2

Write the full words for the contractions.

they're

that's

wouldn't

what'll

who's

we're

hasn't

where's

shouldn't

could've

Challenge 3

Write the correct contractions into the sentences. Then copy the completed sentences.

Mavis ____________ (did'nt / didn't) like strawberries but she ____________ (might've / mightv'e) if she tasted one.

____________ (Ia'm / I'm) going to the fair today; ____________ (I'll / Iw'll) be gone for a while.

He ____________ (shouldv'e / should've) been more careful carrying the plant.

Placing and spacing punctuation: commas and semi-colons

Challenge 1

Copy the sentences, making sure you space the commas correctly.

Tip Commas can be used when describing or listing different things. Semi-colons are often used to separate phrases or instead of using a conjunction such as and, but, so. Semi-colons connect similar ideas.

The train driver collected her keys,lunch,drink and timesheet before she got on the train.

I want bananas,apples,oranges,pears and grapes.

Challenge 2

Copy the sentences, making sure you space the semi-colons correctly.

Tip Read the sentences carefully and see how the semi-colons are used to separate the two main clauses.

She spoke to me yesterday;I told her she could go on the school trip.

Her mother loved to bake;there were always cakes to be eaten.

James liked to climb trees;one day he got stuck on a branch.

Challenge 3

Copy the sentences putting in the semi-colons.

Sally went to her friend's house she was not in.

I have sent out the invites to my party I hope my friends will come.

The meal was cooked we served it to our guests.

Progress check 2

1. Write notes which list the key points of the phone message.

"Hi Arif, so, um... let's meet. Yeah, let's go to the Highways Coffee House. Yeah, there at, um, 2pm. No, 3pm. Yeah. It's on Water Lane. Yeah. Tomorrow. Right?"

2. Copy the sentences, making sure your joins are correct.

Please do not disappear while I am arranging your places.

At night, the town was vividly lit with bright lights.

Put your rulers down on the windowsill.

3. Copy the words. Think carefully about how they should be written.

quads quack

quarry quarter

4. Copy the sentence. Remember to look out for break letters.

Young Fred is a happy, jolly baby.

5. Copy the passage, putting in the correct capital letters and punctuation.

i wasnt very happy. where were my mates i
walked along kicking the leaves i shouldn't have
as i bashed my toe against a stone id had
enough ill go home right now i thought

How I feel about...			
spacing punctuation correctly			
my break letters			
writing brief, detailed notes			

Progress check 2

6. Copy the sentences, putting in any commas and semi-colons that are needed.

Here is a list for you I want laces shoes polish brushes and boots.

The horses galloped down a green straight damp track.

They decided it was too cold to go out they went inside again and played cards all night.

Greg and his friends Konrad John Sean and Jai walked to the football match.

7. Copy the sentences, changing the words to contractions using apostrophes where possible.

I wish I could have gone on holiday because I would like a break from work.

Lexi thinks she is better at running than Edward because he has not been practising.

Ravi did not go out with his friends because he does not like pizza.

How I feel about...	😐	🙂	😀
using apostrophes in contractions			
using commas			
using semi-colons			

Writing quickly 2

Challenge 1

Copy the sentence as quickly as you can.

I have a Gumbie Cat in mind, her name is Jennyanydots; her coat is of the tabby kind, with tiger stripes and leopard spots.

From 'The Old Gumbie Cat' by T. S. Eliot

Challenge 2

You might use mirror writing as a code. Copy the sentence quickly.

I saw you eating cherries off a plate yesterday.

Copy the sentence in mirror writing. How quickly can you write it?

.yadretsey etalp a ffo seirrehc gnitae uoy was I

Make up a sentence of your own. Write it forwards first and then backwards.

Copy the passage as quickly and as legibly as you can.

Tip If you want to improve your writing speed, make sure you are sitting comfortably, holding your pencil correctly and your paper is at the correct angle.

He felt cold, wet and disorientated. Slowly he opened his eyes. Where was he? He was lost and confused. His head ached and his limbs were stiff and painful. He remembered running, pursued by pounding footsteps and loud aggressive yells.

Challenge 3

Copy the passage onto a separate piece of paper, writing quickly and carefully.

A shove and he was falling towards the circle of light that had materialised in front of him. He recalled a voice, his mother's: "Remember us, we love you always." Then silence, darkness – nothing familiar. In fact, nothing that he could recognise as known to him.

From *The Journey* by Shelagh Moore

Writing neatly and printing

Challenge 1

Use the words in the box to print labels on the diagram.

Tip For labelling diagrams, remember to **print** the words clearly.

vent lava ashcloud
magma crater

Challenge 2

Look at the diagram below and how it is labelled. Write the same labels on the diagram on the next page.

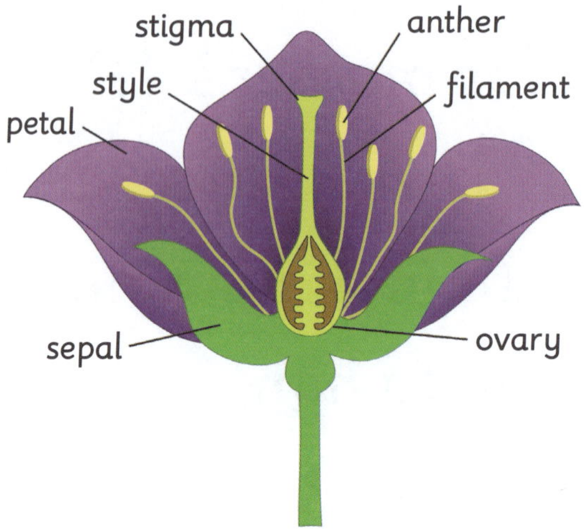
stigma
anther
style
filament
petal
sepal
ovary

Challenge 3

Read the clues, choose the answer and print the letters in the correct boxes in the crossword.

Clues across:

3. Which mammal can blow water into the air when swimming?
5. What flower can tell you the time?
6. A bird calls out and we know it is spring. Name the bird.
7. What contains a joke at Christmas?

Clues down:

1. What did the mouse run up?
2. I spin fine silk to make a trap. What am I?
3. A royal castle outside London.
4. I sell flowers. Who am I?

1
2
3
4
5
6
7

Answers: Across – 3. whale, 5. dandelion, 6. cuckoo, 7. cracker;
Down – 1. clock, 2. spider, 3. Windsor, 4. florist

Alphabetical order

Challenge 1

Copy the words, putting each row in alphabetical order.

switched swirled swithered

pearl peanut peach

exam exasperate exactly

Complete the sentence using words from above. Then copy the completed sentence.

They ______________ the pearl for a painted ______________ which looked ______________ the same as the pearl.

Challenge 2

Copy the words, putting them in alphabetical order.

cuboid cuckoo cucumber cuddle

Write the names in the correct alphabetical order.

Tristan Tristine Trishiv Triestino

Challenge 3

Read the poem. Copy the verse you like best onto a separate piece of paper.

'Twas midnight in the schoolroom
And every desk was shut
When suddenly from the alphabet
Was heard a loud "Tut-Tut!"

Said A to B, "I don't like C;
His manners are a lack.
For all I ever see of C
Is a semi-circular back!"

"I disagree," said D to B,
"I've never found C so.
From where I stand he seems to be
An uncompleted O."

C was vexed, "I'm much perplexed,
You criticise my shape.
I'm made like that, to help spell Cat
And Cow and Cool and Cape."

"He's right" said E; said F, "Whoopee!"
Said G, "'Ip, 'Ip, 'ooray!"
"You're dropping me," roared H to G.
"Don't do it please I pray."

"Out of my way," LL said to K.
"I'll make poor I look ILL."
To stop this stunt J stood in front,
And presto! ILL was JILL.

"U know," said V, "that W
Is twice the age of me.
For as a Roman V is five
I'm half as young as he."

X and Y yawned sleepily,
"Look at the time!" they said.
"Let's all get off to beddy byes."
They did, then "Z-z-z."

'The ABC' by Spike Milligan

Careful writing with break letters

Challenge 1

Copy the sentences carefully.

Tip Think about ascenders, descenders, joins and break letters.

Please persuade your uncle to buy a programme for the match.

He is a professional dancer; it would be a privilege to sit with him at the concert.

Let's hope there is not a long queue.

Challenge 2

The words in each sentence are mixed up. Write the sentences carefully and clearly, with the words in the correct order and adding any punctuation.

love there sufficient in the world never is

must when you apologise mean it you

justice statue the is symbol a of

Challenge 3

Write in the missing words and copy the sentences carefully.

__________ was a cold morning. The __________ was not shining but the __________ was blowing the leaves off the trees.

The __________ were collecting conkers that had __________ onto the ground.

It __________ the conker season and they __________ wanted conkers!

Spacing using compound words

Challenge 1

Copy the compound words carefully.

cartwheel

whiteboard

blackboard

teatime

Draw lines to match the words to make a compound word and then copy the compound words carefully.

cup	ground
back	fish
dough	print
gold	cake
finger	nut

Challenge 2

Copy the passage, making sure you leave a space between each word. Underline the six compound words.

Tip You can use a pencil dot as a guide, or your little finger, to give you an idea of the space between words. Connectors can also be compound words e.g. because, however.

The firefighter jumped into his seat in the fire engine. The driver set the siren wailing and they were off to extinguish the fire. My eardrums were ringing with the sound of the siren. They dashed into the house; the fireguard had been

knocked over and the carpet was smouldering.
An eyewitness, standing in the driveway,
reported that the family had gone shopping.

Challenge 3

Complete the sentences below using the compound words in the box.

eyesight	haircut	grandchildren
eyeglasses	grandparents	hairdresser

My ______________ was poor so I used ______________ to help me see better.

Dad thinks ______________ can have fun with their ______________ especially with sleepovers.

My hair was too long so I went to the ______________ for a ______________.

Slanting your writing

Challenge 1

Copy the letters and then write them in the style you would like to develop.

f g d

b q

Copy the letters of the alphabet as capital letters and then as lower-case letters in your own style.

A B C D E F G H I J K L M N O P Q R S T U V W X Y Z

a b c d e f g h i j k l m n o p q r s t u v w x y z

Challenge 2

Copy the sentences as shown and then in your chosen style.

Frances wanted to join her family on the beach.

They practised making sandcastles and enjoyed a lovely beach picnic.

After an excellent day, the family went home to rest for their trip to the zoo on the next day.

Challenge 3

Copy the sentences in your own style of writing. Think about how you write your ascenders and descenders. They should be parallel to each other.

I liked to walk along the forest paths with my dog.

He was a funny little creature with a quirky nature that made people smile at him.

One hazy day, he disappeared into the woods; I thought I'd lost him but he reappeared further along the path.

Revising key joins: joins to round letters

Challenge 1

Copy each of the round letters three times.

c a d

e g o

p q b

Copy each of the joined round letters three times.

oe ad

dg ng

igh ing

ed cc

dd va

Challenge 2

Copy the words. Think carefully about the joins you use. Underline the vertical joins.

language

ancient

embarrassing

bargain

bruised

sleigh

Copy the sentences.

The rolling countryside with its hills and dales was beautiful to see at sunrise.

Joanna enjoyed swimming as well as walking in the countryside.

Challenge 3

Copy the passage onto a separate piece of paper and add a sentence of your own at the end.

Druke is a baby dragon and Mog is a friendly ogre. Druke grew quickly and liked being with Mog in the garden. He helped Mog weed the garden and plant the seeds. They grew the food they wanted to eat and Druke liked eating the apples!

Spacing tricky joins

Challenge 1

Copy the words.

the we they

are my her

him all

there what

Check your joins and correct any mistakes by writing the word out again.

Challenge 2

Copy the words, making sure that your joins are spaced carefully.

the school

there into

what him

Copy the sentences, making sure that your joins are spaced carefully.

Maia liked to attend school and enjoyed all of her lessons.

However, she still liked holidays best.

Copy the words on the left in joined handwriting. Then draw lines to match each word to the correct synonym for the word that you have copied out. Space your joins carefully.

familiar	signalling
refuge	appear
beckoning	scatter
disperse	shelter
emerge	known

Challenge 3

Copy the poem onto a separate piece of paper. Space any tricky joins carefully.

Who goes there
stopping at my door
in the deep dark dead
of the moonless night?

Who goes there
turning the handle of my door
without a creak or rattle
slowly
round and round?

From 'Hallowe'en Fright' by Robert Fisher

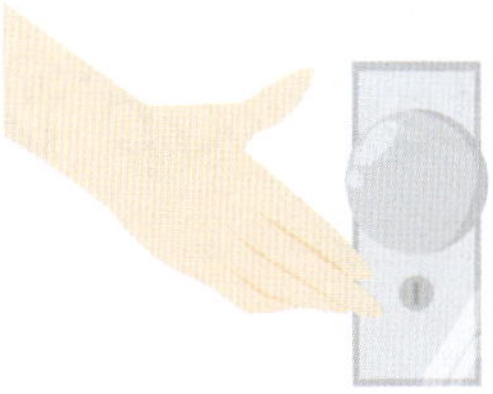

Proofreading and paragraphing

Challenge 1

Identify and underline the incorrect verb, the six spelling errors and two incorrect punctuation marks. Write the passage out correctly.

He were lying under an ancient, giagantic tree, cruched against it's gnarled, twisted root. He was squezed titly under it. He must have crawled into its shelter laast night and sleept in this strange refuge?

Challenge 2

Copy the passage.

A new paragraph begins when you want to move on to a new idea or when you are developing a story or describing a person, place or object. Paragraphs are usually at least four to five sentences long and develop the topic. Paragraphs start on a new line.

Challenge 3

Identify the paragraph break and copy the passage out correctly onto a separate piece of paper.

Tip You are reading the end of one paragraph and the start of the new one. Look for where there is a change of subject.

He had survived the fall uninjured. He was whole but battered and bruised. His skin was already turning purple where the bruising was obvious. A blessing, he thought, as he recalled the events of last night that had led to the flight for his life. The town he had lived in for all of his eleven years had been invaded by terrorists some months ago. They were sworn to destroy a way of life they abhorred and rejected. His town was peaceful; its people were developers of technology that helped them to prosper and be successful.

Progress check 3

1. Copy the sentences quickly and neatly.

Daisy walked in the meadow counting buttercups.

She didn't pick them; she just took photos of them for the nature wall at school.

2. Print the words that you may find on signs.

Price: 50 pence

Jumble Sale today!

EXIT ONLY

FIRE EXIT

ENTRANCE

Hotel Reception

Haircuts – half price today only!

3. Copy the words, putting them into the correct alphabetical order.

soapstone soak soapsuds soapy

SOAP

briny brier bristle bribe brisk

4. Copy the sentences, spacing your words carefully. Underline the compound words.

At the interchange the drivers drove carefully.

We arrived at the mainland and left the boat.

The plane landed on the runway without a jolt.

5. Copy the words in your own writing style.

firefly	gazelle
horizon	quarrel
theatre	porpoise

6. Copy the sentence in your own style.

Jessica, Sofia and Alfonse built a beautiful hideaway in the valley.

How I feel about...			
my printed words			
putting words in alphabetical order			
my style of writing			

Progress check 3

7. Copy the sentences, thinking particularly about how to join the rounded letters.

It was a beautiful day in May. The sun was high in the sky, shining over the tall, old oak tree in the garden. The children sat under the shade of the tree and ate their picnic.

8. Copy the sentences. Space your joins carefully.

The school nurse looked into my eyes as part of my check-up.

"There are so many people about," he said.

She replied, "Well it is the day to go to the market."

9. Proofread the passage and underline any mistakes. Then copy the passage out correctly.

there were a lot of peeple walking towards the

village. Some word red, orange, blue clothes while the other wore grey and browm outfits

10. Identify where the paragraph break should be in the passage. Explain why below.

The boy hid in the undergrowth in the woods. He hoped he had escaped the people following him. He didn't think they would be good to him. Meanwhile, his friends were worried about him. Where was he? They had looked everywhere except the woods. They saw people looking around the woods and realised he must be hiding in them. They hoped his hiding place was safe...

How I feel about...			
my joins in words			
correcting spelling and punctuation mistakes			
identifying paragraph breaks			

Placing and spacing punctuation: commas, dashes and brackets

Challenge 1

Copy the sentences.

Tip Commas, dashes and brackets allow extra information to be added to a sentence to help it make sense.

Pop and Nana (my grandparents) knew the answer.

I unpacked the suitcase – the trousers, socks, shoes towels and wash kit were there but no toothpaste.

Challenge 2

Copy the sentences, putting in the correct capital letters and punctuation.

my friend farid who had walked a long way felt very tired

we were looking up at the building and it was very large when james opened the door and disappeared inside

the laptop was pink bright pink with an even brighter pink cover

Challenge 3

Copy the limerick, making sure you use the same punctuation as the poet.

There was an Old Man with a beard,
Who said, "It is just as I feared!–
Two Owls and a Hen, four Larks and a Wren,
Have all built their nests in my beard!"

'There was an Old Man with a Beard' by Edward Lear

Writing quickly: instructions

Challenge 1

Copy the instructions quickly.

Tip When writing instructions, use short sentences, bullet points and imperative verbs such as go, move, tell, fetch, sit, shut – they tell us what to do.

Go and fetch your brother for his tea.

Line up for your lessons – outside your classrooms – at once!

Challenge 2

Copy the instruction words.

Repeat	Don't
Shut	Write
Switch off	

Write the correct instruction words in the sentences as quickly as you can.

__________ touch the cakes!

__________ your mobile phones in the cinema.

__________ a story about springtime.

__________ after me, "Je m'appelle Tony."

__________ the gate when you leave.

Write some instructions for making a sandwich.

Tip Think about what you need (butter, bread, filling, plate), the order of actions (bullet points or 1, 2, 3) and clear, formal wording.

Challenge 3

Read the nursery rhyme thought to be written by Sarah Catherine Martin (circa 1804).

Old Mother Hubbard
Went to the cupboard,
To give the poor dog a bone:
When she came there,
The cupboard was bare,
And so the poor dog had none.

She went to the baker's
To buy him some bread;
When she came back
The dog was dead!

She went to the undertaker's
To buy him a coffin;
When she came back
The dog was laughing.

She took a clean dish
to get him some tripe;
When she came back
He was smoking his pipe.

On a separate piece of paper, write out some instructions that Mother Hubbard could have been given, such as:

1. Mother Hubbard: Go to the cupboard.
2. Fetch a bone for the dog.

Write three more instructions of your own on a separate piece of paper. Ensure you write quickly and carefully.

Writing neatly

Challenge 1

Copy the words and sentences as neatly as you can.

Tip To write neatly, make sure you have a pen that suits you and that your grip is correct. Sit properly at your table or desk and have your paper slanted correctly. Write carefully in your own style of writing.

leisure

sincerely

necessary

achieve

It was apparent that we would be late for the party at Queen's Gate Lodge.

Giovanni went to the shops to buy his groceries.

Challenge 2

Copy the paragraph from a story about a refugee arriving in a different land to his own.

He hoped these winged people, apparently so different to him, would be hospitable and welcome him. He was terribly weary, he just wanted to sit, have a drink and something to eat. He thought about eating one of his ration packs but decided to wait.

From *The Journey* by Shelagh Moore

Challenge 3

Copy the letter as neatly as you can onto a separate piece of paper. Check all your punctuation and spaces are correct.

Dear Parents

Please remember that the school holidays start on Friday 8 April. The school will be closed for three weeks and open again on 2 May. The school activity, breakfast and lunch club will be open from Monday 11 April until Friday 29 April, from 8.30a.m. until 4.30p.m.

Please make sure you sign up this week if your child wants to attend.

Yours sincerely

M. Jacobs, Headteacher

I want ________________ (child's name) in Class ______ (Class)

to attend the Activity Club from _______ until ____________ (put in dates)

Signed _______________ Parent/Carer

Proofreading

Challenge 1

Copy the sentence, correcting any punctuation errors.

please buy some apples oranges and grapes instructed the children

Challenge 2

Read the following paragraph and underline the mistakes, then write the paragraph correctly. There are 11 spelling and punctuation errors.

Aunt beatrice walked slowly along the road she wanted to let her grandson catch up with her. He had just learnt to todle and was qite slow She turned round and smiled at him. What a seet cild he was she thouht he would like a treet when they got to the park

Copy the conversation, putting in the missing punctuation.

Are you ready to go asked Adnan

Id like to get my bag first replied Alice

Its here said her mum bringing in her bag and handing it to her

Thanks mum that's great I can go now Alice hugged her mum and left with Adnan

Challenge 3

Proofread the passage and underline the 14 errors you find. Copy the corrected passage onto a separate piece of paper.

I like walking to see my nan. She live in a diferent part ot towm. Her stret has trees, bencehs and planter with flours in them I think it's a pretty place to live she does to. At nans ill get sum cake!

Neatest writing: break letters, ascenders and descenders

Challenge 1

Copy the sentences.

I enjoyed the event enormously.

The food was really delicious.

I saw that the children loved the Punch and Judy show.

Challenge 2

Copy the sentences with tricky joins and spacing.

The dentist examined my teeth very thoroughly.

The greengrocers sold every variety of apple.

Mason's mum checked his temperature.

Challenge 3

Write a short letter to thank Mrs Ali, who found your wallet.

POLICE

Note writing: abbreviations and contractions

Challenge 1

Write out the abbreviations and contractions in full.

should've

DIY

adj.

couldn't

Challenge 2

Copy the sentences, putting in the abbreviations and contractions.

I am looking for a job at the British Broadcasting Corporation.

Doctor Foster was a Member of Parliament for Gloucester.

I would like the results as soon as possible.

Challenge 3

Copy the passage, writing the abbreviations and contractions in full.

We're going to Brighton for our hols. I'm hoping that the weather will be warm and sunny as there'll be lots of walking to do. I've watched tv programmes and know you need waterproofs, good walking shoes and a backpack at least. Mr Dunn told us at school that walking was good for your health. There have been programmes on the BBC about walking. I'm hoping my DIY walking kit will be useful on the holiday.

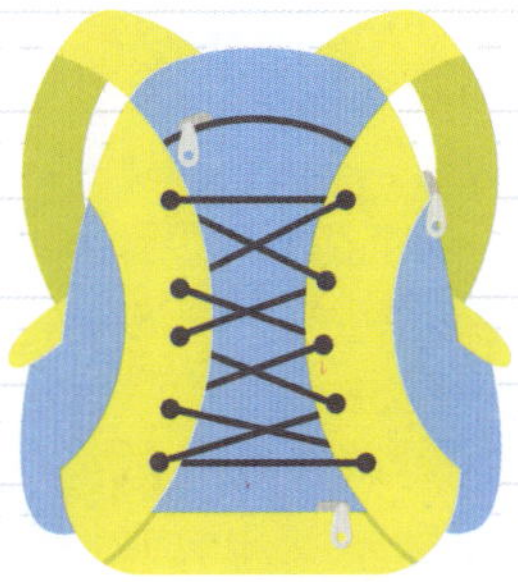

Writing quickly and legibly

Challenge 1

Copy out these common sayings.

A stitch in time saves nine.

More haste, less speed.

An apple a day keeps the doctor away.

One good turn deserves another.

V

Challenge 2

Write a quick summary of this account.

A young man sped very quickly around the corner of Lambeth Road on a Seedigo scooter. Another rider came around the corner of Lambeth Road riding carefully. They collided when one of the young men swerved his scooter to avoid a cat. The cat fortunately escaped unharmed after avoiding a bus and three cars. The two young men then had a noisy argument but were unharmed, if somewhat shocked.

Challenge 3

Write out the conversation, making it sound as interesting as possible.

You were going too fast!
Jay
You were on the wrong side of the road!
Rav
They shot round the corner!
Is anyone hurt?

Writing beautifully

Challenge 1

Copy the tongue twisters.

She sells seashells on the seashore.

Round the rugged rock the ragged rascal ran.

I scream, you scream, we all scream for
ice cream.

Challenge 2

Write an invitation using these details.

12.00, Sparrow's Rest, High St, birthday, Lukas,
Nov 12th

Event:

Who:

Place:

Date:

Time:

Challenge 3

Copy the poem in your neatest handwriting.

He clasps the crag with crooked hands;
Close to the sun in lonely lands,
Ring'd with the azure world, he stands.
The wrinkled sea beneath him crawls;
He watches from his mountain walls,
And like a thunder bolt he falls.

'The Eagle' by Alfred, Lord Tennyson

Progress check 4

1. Copy the sentences, putting in the commas, dashes and brackets.

We need seeds compost a watering can and a trowel from the garden centre.

I would like you to get me some wool blue yellow and green balls so that I can finish my knitting.

Grass and wildflowers loved by bees grew very tall in the field

2. Copy the sentences quickly.

Go and answer the telephone!

"Plant the seeds here," instructed my teacher.

"Tidy your bedroom," she was told by her sister.

3. Copy the passage as neatly as you can.

It was spring and Adam and his grandma were in a shop that sold lots of different things.

"What are you looking for Grandma?" asked Adam. "I want to get some seeds that will grow into pretty flowers for our plant pots," Grandma replied. Adam spotted a packet of wildflower seeds. "I wonder what they will be like," he said, hoping that Grandma would buy them.

How I feel about...	😐	🙂	😃
using commas, dashes and brackets			
writing quickly and neatly			

Progress check 4

4. Copy the words, making sure your ascenders and descenders are parallel.

dreary diary greatly the terrified

unfriendly dispute hello aggravate

5. Copy the sentence, making sure your ascenders and descenders are parallel.

The giraffe looked at the sky, the tree and the water before he bowed his very long neck to the water and began to drink.

6. Copy the words, putting them into the correct alphabetical order.

thatch thimble thistle

lawyer lawgiver lawfully

flourish flour flouncing

FLOUR

7. Print the words.

gather

eating

yanking

xylophone

march

joining

zebras

shiny

8. Copy the words in your own writing style.

gather

march

eating

joining

zebras

How I feel about...	😐	🙂	😀
my ascenders and descenders			
putting words into alphabetical order			
my own writing style			

Progress chart

Draw ticks in the boxes to show how you feel about your handwriting.

	Not sure	Working on it	I can do it!
My descenders and ascenders			
Using punctuation			
My joins			
My quick writing			
My neat writing			
Spacing punctuation correctly			
My break letters			
Writing brief, detailed notes			
Using apostrophes in contractions			
Using commas			
Using semi-colons			
My printed words			
Putting words in alphabetical order			
My style of writing			
My joins in words			
Correcting spelling and punctuation mistakes			
Identifying paragraph breaks			
Using commas, dashes and brackets			
Placing speech marks around direct speech			